For Tim, Noa and Dustin

~ Hanako Clulow

360 DEGREES
An imprint of the Little Tiger Group
www.littletiger.co.uk
1 Coda Studios, 189 Munster Road,
London SW6 6AW
First published in Great Britain 2016
Text by Patricia Hegarty
and Tanera Simons
Text copyright © Caterpillar Books Ltd. 2016
Illustrations copyright
© Hanako Clulow 2016

ISBN: 978-1-84857-504-2
CPB/1800/1059/1118
3 4 5 6 7 8 9 10

# ABOVE and BELOW

Illustrated by Hanako Clulow

360 degrees

# The Ocean

Oceans cover 71% of the Earth's surface and they play a major part in our climate and weather systems. But did you know that more than 95% of the underwater world remains unexplored? That leaves plenty for us to discover!

## coral

Coral reefs take millions of years to form. Coral organisms are actually translucent; they get their bright hues from the billions of colourful algae they host.

## palm tree

As well as coconuts, different species of palm tree produce a wide variety of fruits.

## loggerhead turtle

Females dig a hole in the sand, lay their eggs, then return to the sea. On hatching, the babies must fend for themselves.

## starfish

Starfish don't have brains or blood! If necessary, they can re-grow their limbs.

## dolphin

Dolphins are very sociable creatures and use squeaks and whistles to communicate with each other.

## albatross

The albatross has the largest wingspan of any bird – up to 3.4m – and it can glide for hours without resting.

## crab

There are over 4,500 species of crab, living in both oceans and fresh water.

## flying fish

This species of fish has evolved to be able to 'fly' as a way of escaping from predators below the water.

### sloth

Sloths sleep for 15–20 hours each day. They are so slow-moving that green algae grow on their furry coats!

### monarch butterfly

These amazing creatures undertake a mass migration of up to 5,000km each winter, to fly to sunnier climes.

### python

Pythons use chemical receptors in their tongues to stalk prey, which they are able to swallow whole.

### leaf-cutter ant

The leaf-cutter ant's jaw vibrates at a rate of 1,000 times per second, allowing it to cut through leaves quickly.

### toucan

Although famous for their colourful bills, toucans are not born with them – they develop as the toucan grows.

# The Rainforest

There are two types of rainforest: temperate and tropical. The difference between rainforests and jungles is that the thick canopies of trees in rainforests block out light, whereas jungles let in more light. The Amazon is the world's largest tropical rainforest.

### leaves

Leaves form a vitally important part of the rainforest: its canopy, which houses a hugely diverse range of creatures.

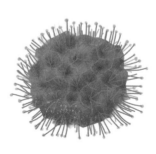

### powderpuff flower

This flower, blooming in winter and spring, attracts butterflies and hummingbirds.

### alpinia flower

The alpinia flower is actually a member of the ginger family.

### quetzal

During mating season, male quetzals grow twin tail feathers, forming an incredible train which grows up to 1m long.

### parrot

'Parrot' covers a broad order of more than 350 birds, including macaws, amazons, lorikeets, lovebirds, and cockatoos.

### spider monkey

The spider monkey's long arms and tail are ideal for gripping branches, allowing it to swing nimbly from tree to tree.

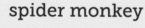

### tree frog

The red-eyed tree frog developed its bright scarlet eyes in order to shock and scare away predators.

er
guars
hers,
, turtles
ns.

# The North Pole

The North Pole is the northernmost point of the Earth and sits in the middle of the Arctic Ocean. In winter, temperatures can drop as low as -43°C, and many animals migrate south to warmer climates. Those that remain have often developed special features to help them survive.

### ice floe

Ice floes are flat masses of free-moving ice that float on the surface of the ocean.

### iceberg

Icebergs, in contrast, are large masses of ice that have broken away from glaciers or ice shelves, and are not normally flat. The North Atlantic and Antarctic regions contain the largest number of icebergs in the world.

### snowy owl

Unlike most other species of owl, snowy owls are not nocturnal – they are active and hunt both day and night.

### walrus

The walrus is capable of slowing its heartbeat to help withstand the freezing polar temperatures.

### polar bear

Under their fur, polar bears have black skin – this helps them to absorb the warmth of the sun's rays.

### arctic fox

Arctic foxes live in burrows and can tunnel deep into the snow to survive the Arctic's icy temperatures.

### ermine

In the summer months the ermine's fur is reddish brown, and in the winter it turns almost completely white.

### snow goose

Snow geese fly in V-formation to reduce wind drag and risk of collision.

### porpoise

Porpoises are among the smallest marine mammals. They have 60–120 teeth, which are flattened into a spade-like shape at the tip.

### orca

One of the world's most powerful predators, the orca's teeth can grow up to 10cm in length.

### narwhal

Nicknamed 'the unicorn of the sea', narwhals are famous for the large tusk on their heads. This 'tusk' is actually a tooth that grows right through their lips, and can reach lengths of up to 2.7m.

### planktonic copepod

Planktonic copepods are tiny aquatic crustaceans.

### harp seal

Spending relatively little time on land, the harp seal is an adept swimmer, feeding on fish and crustaceans.

### arctic cod

This cod lives farther north than any other marine fish.

### humpback whale

The humpback whale has grooves on it throat, allowing it to expand when it feeds.

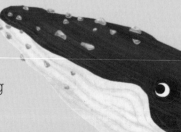

# The River

Freshwater rivers and streams and their riverbanks are home to a huge array of wildlife. Some species thrive in deep, fast-flowing water, while others make their homes in spots where the water moves more slowly.

### oak tree
The fruit of an oak tree, the acorn, is not produced until the tree reaches around 40 years of age.

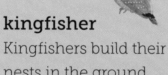

### lily pad
Water lilies grow in slow-moving water, providing valuable shelter for fish and other creatures.

### bulrushes
Bulrushes grow largely in shallow water, reaching heights of up to 3m.

### willow tree
The willow is one of the fastest growing trees in the world, growing by as much as 3m in a year.

### stoat
Often confused with weasels, stoats are larger, and have a longer, black-tipped tail. A group of stoats is called a 'caravan'.

### kingfisher
Kingfishers build their nests in the ground, often in a vertical bank, just above the water. This helps to protect them from predators.

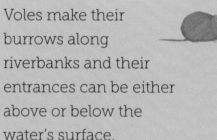

### vole
Voles make their burrows along riverbanks and their entrances can be either above or below the water's surface.

### coot
Webbed feet help the coot when swimming and walking on slippery riverbanks.

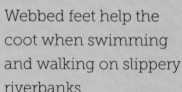

### swan
A male swan is called a cob and the female a pen. Swans are among the few creatures that mate for life.

### frog
Frogs lay their eggs (spawn) in water. These hatch into tadpoles, which in turn become fully-grown frogs.

### dragonfly
Dragonflies move like helicopters – both up and down, as well as sideways.

### perch

Perch have two dorsal fins; the first is spiny and the second is soft-rayed.

### pearl mussel

Pearl mussels can reach ages of up to 100 years, but their numbers are declining due to illegal pearl fishing.

### dace

Blacknose dace are distinguished by a dark lateral line along the body.

### trout

Trout can be very territorial, often chasing other trout off their patch!

### snail

The snail's shell is part of its body and helps to protect it against predators.

### eel

Despite their snake-like appearance, eels are fish, not reptiles. Some species grow up to 2m in length.

### otter

Otters eat mainly fish, but their sharp teeth mean they can bite into animals with shells such as crabs and snails.

### pike

Female pikes are often the largest predator in their habitat, reaching up to 1.8m in length.

### water beetle

Most water beetles are also adept fliers, allowing them to colonise new ponds and source more food.

### screech owl
As well as screeches, these owls make sounds including rasps, barks, hoots, chuckles and trills.

### flying squirrel
Flying squirrels glide through the air across distances of up to 90m.

### bald eagle
The bald eagle is not actually bald – its head is covered in white feathers, giving it its distinctive appearance.

### wild boar
The wild boar is extremely adaptable, eating almost anything it can fit in its mouth.

### wild turkey
A wild turkey's distinctive 'gobbling' sound can be heard up to 1.6km away. What noisy neighbours!

### ruby-throated hummingbird
The 'hum' of a hummingbird comes from the rapid beating of its wings.

### bobcat
Fierce hunters, bobcats can kill prey much bigger than themselves.

# Mountain Caves

Rocky mountain ranges are often riddled with caves, and such nooks and crannies are the perfect hideout for secretive species. Natural warmth makes caves a popular home for animals, some of which are specially adapted to cope in the dark.

### mountain laurel
The mountain laurel is an evergreen shrub, often found in rocky or mountainous areas. Be careful – it's poisonous!

### wild flowers
Wild flowers grow naturally in their environment, without human care.

### buddleia
Buddleia shrubs are often called 'butterfly' bushes, because they attract a large number of butterflies.

# Savannah

The hot, dry savannah has an open canopy, with trees spaced widely enough to allow grasslands to develop. Often, rainfall is confined to one season, meaning that water is scarce during the dry months. Wildlife must adapt to survive in these extreme conditions.

### savannah grass
There are hundreds of different types of grass growing in the African savannah, which are drought-resistant and hardy.

### baobab tree
Baobab trees have distinctive swollen trunks, which are used for storing huge amounts of water.

### guarri bush
The guarri is considered a highly valuable plant, used for medicinal purposes to treat conditions as diverse as leprosy and tooth decay.

### giraffe
The giraffe is the world's tallest mammal. Its markings are unique – like human fingerprints.

### peacock
Male peacocks are famous for their huge trains of tail feathers, which can reach up to 2m in length.

### rhinoceros
A rhino's tough skin is 1.5cm thick. Its horn is made of keratin, like a human's fingernail.

### lion
Lions are the only species of cat that live in social groups, known as prides.

### elephant
An elephant's trunk is actually a very long nose, used for grabbing things, as well as for breathing and smelling.

### flamingo
Flamingos have a distinctive pink colouring, which is due to their diet of shrimp-like crustaceans.

### gazelle
Gazelles can run at speeds of up to 97kph in short bursts.

own to
help their
and to aid
water.

are a main source
od for many
nnah creatures.

### mongoose

The mongoose lives in an underground burrow. Some species are semi-aquatic.

### zebra

Zebras have unique markings, meaning that no two zebras have the same stripes.

### snake

There are more than 2,700 species of snake living in all sorts of habitats.

### gecko

Most geckos cannot blink, but they lick their eyes to keep them moist.

### ostrich

The ostrich, the world's largest bird, can't fly but it can run at 80kph!

### bull frog

Bull frogs make a very distinctive loud, deep bellowing sound.

### scorpion

Scorpions have existed on Earth for over 400 million years – they are even older than the dinosaurs!

### whale

There are many different species of whale, divided into two main groups: baleen whales and toothed whales. They live in groups called pods. In order to breathe, they have blowholes on the tops of their heads.

### seal

The seal has two layers of thick fur and a warm layer of fat called blubber to keep it warm in the icy waters in which it lives.

### gull

Seagulls are very clever birds, able to learn and pass on certain behaviours. They will drop hard-shelled molluscs onto rocks to break them open for their lunch!

# The Clifftops

Cliffs are usually formed of rock that is resistant to erosion and weathering such as sandstone, chalk and limestone. They can often be found in the most remote and isolated parts of the world. Some creatures form colonies which thrive in rocky outcrops and cliff faces, using the ocean as their feeding ground.

### puffin burrow

Puffins build their nests at the end of burrows that are up to 1m long. They dig these burrows using their bills and feet to shovel out dirt. They are designed to keep their chicks safe from predators.

### lichen

Lichen, unlike most living things, doesn't consist of a single organism. It is formed by two co-existing 'partners': a fungus and an alga.

# The Forest

Forests are large areas of land covered with trees and woody vegetation. They are home to all kinds of wildlife, from tiny insects to nesting birds and rodents to ruminant mammals. Under the ground there is a maze of tree roots, burrows and warrens providing homes for many of the creatures.

### toadstool
A toadstool is a fleshy fungus, with a cap and a stem.

### beech tree
Both male and female flowers are found on the same tree – making beech trees 'monoecious'.

### tree roots
A tree's roots can spread up to three times the height of the tree, obtaining water, oxygen, and minerals from the soil.

### woodpecker
Woodpeckers use their hard, chisel-shaped beaks to carve holes out of tree trunks, where they make their nests.

### deer
The male deer sheds and regrows its antlers every year. Their size varies with the age of the deer, and increases annually over several years before reaching maximum size.

### robin
The robin is a member of the thrush family. Most pairs of robins will produce three broods of chicks per year.

### badger
Badgers are nocturnal, preferring to hunt for their favourite food – earthworms – at night. They can eat up to 200 earthworms every day!

### hedgehog
The hedgehog protects itself from predators by curling up into a ball, leaving only its spikes exposed – a very effective deterrent!

### nesting bird
A bird's nest is where it lays and incubates its eggs. They are often made of interwoven twigs and grass.

### red squirrel
Squirrels do not hibernate, but bury a good supply of nuts and seeds in the ground to see them through the winter.